**UBU
TRUMP**

UBU TRUMP

A Drama in Five Acts in Prose

By Alfred Jarry

First Performed By The Marionettes
Of *The Theatre Of Finances** In 1888.

Translated And Entirely Updated
By **Rosanna Hildyard** in 2017

EYEWEAR PUBLISHING

* The
'Théâtre de Phynances'
was the name Jarry gave
to the shows he produced
from his marionette
theatre while a school-
boy at *lycée*.

First published in 2017
by Eyewear Publishing Ltd
Suite 333, 19-21 Crawford Street
Marylebone, London W1H 1PJ
United Kingdom

Cover design and typeset by Edwin Smet
Cover and interior drawings by Rosanna Hildyard
Edited and proofread by Alexandra Payne & Todd Swift
Printed in England by TJ International Ltd, Padstow, Cornwall

ISBN 978-1-911335-93-1

Eyewear wishes to thank Jonathan Wonham for his
generous patronage of our press.

WWW.EYEWEARPUBLISHING.COM

THIS BOOK
is dedicated to
MARCEL RUPERT SCHWOB
Allusive, baroque, exotic; Schwob (1867-1905)
was a French symbolist writer and friend of Jarry's.
Among other things, Schwob had a passion for slang,
believing that it was not a spontaneous exclamation
but a form of artificial language or code.

And, at the gracious nod of *King Ubu's* golden-haloed head, we can *now reveal*, ladies and gentlemen, that the writer claimed by the 'English' to be their so-called 'Shakespeare', was actually *our very own Ubu*, who under that pseudonym authored – and this is God's honest truth, ladies and gentlemen – the great tragedies *Macbeth, Hamlet* and *Julius Caesar* – and *handwritten*.

CHARACTERS

UBU – *later* KING
MAMA UBU
CAPTAIN BORDURE
GOOD KING WENCESLAS
QUEEN ROSAMUND
Their three sons:
BOLESLAW
LAIDISLAW
CROWN PRINCE BUGGERLAW
TSAR VLADIMIR OF RUSSIA
AMERICAN GENERAL

Trumpeters:
TRASHTAG
TRITE
TRILLANY

MERCENARIES *and* SOLDIERS
PEOPLE
LITTLE DONALD THE MARATHON RUNNER
NOBLES
MAGISTRATES
ADVISORS
BANKERS
BANKERS' MINIONS
PEASANTS
THE WHOLE RUSSIAN ARMY
THE WHOLE AMERICAN ARMY

MAMA UBU'S GUARDS
BEAR
HORSE
THE DESTROYING MACHINE
SHIP'S CAPTAIN
SHIP'S CREW

PREFACE

The task of translating *Ubu Roi* into *Ubu Trump* was continually self-justifiying. As I plodded through each scene, sitting in the library with a scrawled-on copy by my side, each page seemed to make a fresh comment on contemporary American politics. For example, I was translating Ubu's derogatory behaviour towards his wife at the same time as the allegations of his sexual assaults were coming out. His order 'Through the trapdoor with the magistrates!' came at the time Trump revealed his controversial list of nominees to the Supreme Court, amid accusations that he was skewing the US justice system. Delicate Queen Rosamund's concern for her upper-class bloodline suggested, when transposed to a US setting, that her Presidential family were just one more of the elite political dynasties that Trump's supporters were sick of – the Kennedys, the Bushes, the Clintons. Well, Trump didn't spring from Cape Cod or Harvard Law School, and has been snubbed for not taking the established route into politics. *Ubu Roi* was almost too easy to make modern.

However, I wanted to rewrite this play, not just translate it. So, while the plot and most of the language follows Jarry's French, much is added. For example, in the Poland of *Ubu Roi,* Wenceslas scolds Buggerlaw for rudeness towards a member of the nobility:

LE ROI: Monsieur Bougrelas, vous avez été ce matin fort impertinent avec Monsieur Ubu, chevalier de mes ordres et comte de Sandomir. C'est pourquoi je vous défends de paraître à ma revue.

[KING: Mr Buggerlaw, this morning you were extremely rude to Mr Ubu, my knight and Count of Sandomir. For this reason, I'm forbidding you from appearing at my parade.]

It was easy for me to extrapolate from this and see in Ubu the CEO who gives financial backing to American politicians today:

KING: Buggerlaw, this morning you were exceedingly rude about Mr Ubu, a member of Congress and a businessman whose donations are extremely important to the administration's campaigns. For this reason, I forbid you to appear at the charity fundraising gala today.

Political administrations have to keep their supporters sweet; a celebrity billionaire is a valuable asset to any politician and must not be offended by an upstart delegate.

Trump's language on Twitter and in speech is littered with the same words and phrases. Insults: 'weak', 'sad', 'pathetic', 'loser'; superlatives: 'totally', 'very', 'major', '100%', 'no', 'means nothing'; exclamations: 'Sad!' 'Pathetic!'; egotistical patting on the back: 'I think I am a good person,' 'I'm winning!' 'I'd beat him', 'I know all about'. I hope the continuities between this speech and my Ubu's are clear.

However, *Ubu Trump* is not just a joke about Trump – *look, a fat, vain dramatic character from an old Surrealist play resembles the current President!* It is also a translation of a drama that is still provocative and relevant to our cultural zeitgeist. Aside from the Trump aspect, *Ubu Roi* stands as a satire on the abuse of power, an irreverent parody of Shakespeare, and a significant influence on Absurdism (Yeats, Beckett) and Dadaism. In it, Jarry was doing something new with dramatic language – challenging the conventional and offending almost everyone who came to see the play. Audiences expected plot and high culture, they got nonsensical action and jokes about shit.

In fact, this new translation of *Ubu Roi* brings to an English-speaking audience the archetypal figure the Western world fears above all: the brute. Ubu and *Ubu* mock civilisation itself; in the form of foreign kings and royal bloodlines, yes, but also with crude language and the insolent, almost savage attitude the play strikes towards its refined audience. It shocks us out of cultural complacency. And it is still, justifiably, as furious in effect when it is performed today.

Rosanna Hildyard, London, 11th July 2017

PERFORMANCE RIGHTS

Applications for performance, including readings and excerpts, by amateurs and professionals in the English language should be addressed to Eyewear Publishing, Suite 333, 19-21 Crawford Street, London, W1H 1PJ, email info@eyewearpublishing.com. No performance of any kind may be given unless a licence has been obtained. Applications should be made before rehearsals begin. Publication of this play does not necessarily indicate its availability for performance.

ACT I
SCENE I
UBU, MAMA UBU

UBU   Oh, SHIT!

MAMA UBU   Well, that's a fine thing to hear, Daddy Ubu. My, you must be some kinda tough guy, shooting your mouth off like that.

UBU   You watch out – I'll get you locked up!

MAMA UBU   It isn't me you've got to lock up, Ubu. Shouldn't you be thinking about locking up someone else ... for good!?

Pause.

UBU   Uh, I don't follow.

MAMA UBU   Ubu, how come you're satisfied with what you are?

UBU   Well, ma'am, why wouldn't I be satisfied? My kids are good-looking, I have a great company, I have a tremendous income. I'm Captain of the Dragoons, Advisor to the King, multi-billionaire tycoon producer of *The Apprentice*. Why, I'm winning!

MAMA UBU   What! So, after building a multi-million dollar golf, hotel and casino empire, buying the *Miss Universe* contest, producing *The Apprentice*, becoming the 324th richest man in the United States, being nominated for an Emmy Award and earning a star on the Hollywood Walk of Fame, you're content to stay just that? What are you – some kind of a loser? When you could reach out and grab *the White House* by the balls?

UBU   Mama Ubu, you're talking but I don't understand what you're saying.

MAMA UBU Oh, you are so dumb!

UBU   King Wenceslas is the King – and even if he wasn't, there are millions more politicians. Why, I've seen 'em!

MAMA UBU What's stopping us from massacring all of them and putting you in their place?

UBU   What! What is going on with you? You're disregarding our safety! Next thing you know, you're going to get the CIA on us!

MAMA UBU Ooh! The CIA! Poor little Ubu! And if I was locked up by the CIA, who'd wash your shitty panties then?

UBU   So what about my panties? Everyone shits, they can't exactly hide it.

MAMA UBU If I were you, I'd take my shitty ass up to the White House, and sit it right down in the Oval Office. Just think…if you did, you could just go on and on getting richer and richer, eating burgers every day, people applauding you wherever you go, driving through the streets in a limousine with tinted windows…

UBU   …Mmm, I could get myself a new wig – let the haters hate!

MAMA UBU You could get as many wigs as you wanted, and lots of shiny badges, a special Royal golf suit…

UBU   Okay, I give in. I tell you, let me just spend fifteen minutes with King Wenceslas down a dark alley at night, and I'd show him. I'd beat him. Hands down.

MAMA UBU Well, Ubu, *now* you're talking like a man!

UBU Oh. Jesus! Me, a fake-tanned celebrity-showman hotel-mogul, kill the King of the United States of America!? I couldn't! It's ridiculous!

MAMA UBU *(aside)* Oh, jeez. *(to Ubu)* So you'd rather stay a loser, Ubu?

UBU Well, Goddammit, I'd rather stay as I am – poor, handsome and honourable – than rich and a bad person. I think I am a good person!

MAMA UBU And the badges? And the royal golf suit? And the new wig?

UBU *(pointing his finger at her)* You, ma'am, are a disgrace to our country.

Ubu stomps offstage, slamming the door petulantly after him.

MAMA UBU *(alone)* Goddamn it! He's more stubborn than I thought. But I think I've shaken him. If it's God's will – and mine – then, all being well, in one week's time I should be Queen of the United States...

SCENE II

UBU, MAMA UBU

The lavishly overdecorated dining room of a suite in Ubu Tower. Leather everywhere. Furniture displays the logos of Fendi, Armani and Versace. A mahogany table is laid with a sumptuous spread of Mexican food: tacos, tortillas, burritos, enchiladas, steaks, burgers, etc.

MAMA UBU Ugh, our guests are late. That is so rude.

UBU   Yeah, jeez. What slobbish and vulgar
             people. I'm starving here! Speaking
             of food, you've been looking pretty chubby
             lately. You trying to show me up in front
             of our guests or something?

MAMA UBU Fuck off.

UBU   *(seizing a cheeseburger)* Hell, I'm hungry. I
             can't wait any longer for these mother-
             fuckers. Look at this burger. Isn't this the
             most beautiful cheeseburger you've ever
             seen? I think our chef makes the best
             cheeseburgers in this city – and I know
             a lot about cheeseburgers.

MAMA UBU What are you doing, you moron! What are
             our guests going to eat?

UBU   *(through a mouthful of cheeseburger)* They'll get

enough... I won't touch any more, I
promise. I promise, I promise, I promise!
Look, why don't you go look out the
window and see if our guests have arrived?

MAMA UBU *(going over to window)* I don't see anyone.

*While she goes to the window, Ubu grabs a burrito and starts
stuffing it into his mouth.*

MAMA UBU Ooh! Here comes Captain Bordure and a
couple of his bootlickers. *(turns around to
catch Ubu seizing a steak with his bare
hands)* What! What are you doing?

UBU   Doing! I've done nothing. It's a lie.

MAMA UBU You *asshole*! The steak, the steak, the steak!
You've ruined the fucking – *(UBU leaps to
his feet, threatening her with his steak
knife)* – States!

UBU   Listen, you motherfucker, if you don't
shut the fuck up I'm going to beat the
hell out of you! Supremacist style!

ALFRED JARRY / ROSANNA HILDYARD

SCENE III
THE SAME

The door opens. Ubu jumps behind it in fright, as Mama composes herself. Enter CAPTAIN BORDURE and SOLDIERS.

MAMA UBU   Welcome, Mr Captain, why, we've been so impatient to meet you! Why don't you take a seat.

CAPTAIN   Good evening, ma'am. But whereabouts is Mr Ubu?

UBU   *(jumping out awkwardly)* I'm here! I'm here! Can't you sense my awesome presence? I'm worth $8 billion, don't you know?

CAPTAIN   *(to Ubu)* Good evening, sir. *(to his followers)* Sit down, men.

They all sit.

UBU   Hmph. This chair is a bit tight. What's wrong with it?

CAPTAIN   So! Mrs Ubu, what delights have you prepared for us today?

MAMA UBU   Here's the menu.

UBU   *(snatching it)* Oh, that's interesting.

MAMA UBU   Enchiladas, tacos, cheese, guacamole, chicken mole, salsa, chipotle steak, steak, more tacos, cheeseburgers, cheese...

UBU   Hm. It'll have to do, I guess... Well? Is there any more?

MAMA UBU   Hamburgers, chips, burritos, cheese, sour cream, cheese, salad.

UBU   What the hell? Do you think I'm some kind of millionaire, to spend so much on one dinner?

MAMA UBU   Don't listen to him, gentlemen, he's an imbecile.

UBU   Agh! I'm gonna hit you harder'n you've ever been hit before!

MAMA UBU   Shut up and eat, Papa Ubu. Here, have a taco.

UBU   Your tacos taste like shit.

CAPTAIN   Well, that wouldn't taste very nice! Heh, heh, heh!

MAMA UBU   *(leaping up from the table)* You bunch of

imbeciles! What do you want to eat, then?

UBU   *(patting his belly)* Oh! I've got an idea! I'll be right back.

He leaves.

MAMA UBU Gentlemen, I'd love for you all to try the steak.

CAPTAIN   It was great, honey, but I'm done.

MAMA UBU *(menacingly)* You'll try some rump steak, Captain. Try rump. *Try rump.*

CAPTAIN   *(nervously eating the offered steak)* Well, now, that's exquisite. Three cheers for Mama Ubu, men!

MEN   Hip hip, hooray! Hip hip, hooray! Hip hip –

Ubu re-enters.

UBU   What's all this? Why aren't you cheering for me?

In his hand he holds an indescribably filthy mop and bucketful of dirty water. He throws it over the table.

MAMA UBU Ubu! What the hell are you doing?

UBU   Why don't you have some more food,
           everyone! Ha, ha!

A few men try the food and instantly fall down, poisoned.

UBU   Mama Ubu, pass me the guacamole. I'll
           serve.

MAMA UBU Here.

UBU   Now get out, all of you! Captain Bordure,
           I want to talk with you.

MEN   What! But we didn't get any food.

UBU   The hell, you didn't get any food! Get out!
           Stay, Bordure.

Nobody moves.

UBU   You aren't going? Well, if you aren't going,
           I'm going to give you your food, alright!

He begins hurling food at them.

MEN   Ow! Ow! Help! Defend us! Murder! He's
           killing us!

UBU   Get out, assholes! The door! Ubu is making
               himself very clear.

MEN   Save us! Ubu lied to us!

They flee offstage.

UBU   I can't resist hitting them because they're
               just so pathetic and easy. Stupid! Wow, my
               heart is beating fast. I've made us safe, but
               that wasn't one of my better dinners,
               Mama. Come, Bordure.

SCENE IV – THE SAME
UBU, MAMA UBU, BORDURE

UBU   Well, Captain, did you enjoy dinner?

CAPTAIN   Very much, sir, except for the shit you
               threw on it.

UBU   Huh! My shit wasn't so bad.

MAMA UBU Each to his own.

UBU   Captain, I've decided to appoint you as
               Duke of California.

CAPTAIN   How's that? I didn't know you were that
               high up in the government. I thought you

were just a celebrity businessman.

UBU   Yes, but I'm the only one that can beat
                Wenceslas. And in a couple of days,
                the American people are going to be
                cheering for *me* as their King.

CAPTAIN   How are you gonna beat Wenceslas?

UBU   *(to audience)* He's not dumb, this guy –
                he's got straight to the point.

CAPTAIN   If this is about killing Wenceslas, I'm in.
                I hate the guy. And I'll vouch for my men
                as well.

UBU   *(throwing himself on Bordure and kissing him)*
                Oh! Oh! I love you, Captain!

CAPTAIN   *(clawing at Ubu in an effort to get away from
                him)* Oh my God! You smell bad, man! Do
                you never wash, or what?

UBU   Well, rarely.

MAMA UBU Never.

UBU   I'm the one who decides how often I wash –
                not you, not anyone else!

MAMA UBU You're not just talking out of your ass —
you are a talking rectum!

UBU You can go now, Bordure, we're done here.
But by the power of Ubu Tower, I swear to
you, with my wife as a witness, that you'll
be the Duke of California.

MAMA UBU But —

UBU Shut up.

They exit.

SCENE V
The Ubus' Bedroom
PAPA UBU, MAMA UBU in bed, snoring.
Enter MESSENGER, who coughs to wake them.

UBU *(to Messenger)* I fell asleep watching The
Emmys. I already know all the winners.
What do you want, anyway?

MESSENGER Sir, you've been called for an audience
with the King.

Exit Messenger.

UBU Shit! Oh fucking shit! My ass, I've been
found out! I'm gonna be locked up!
I'm gonna be waterboarded in Alcatraz!

OhmyGodohmyGodohmyGod...

MAMA UBU *(waking up)* Oh, what a loser. Stop
panicking, time is short!

UBU   Wait! I'll just blame it all on Mama Ubu
and Bordure.

MAMA UBU What! You fat worm, if you say that, I'll —

UBU   Hey, it's all going to be OK! I'll just head to
the White House now.

Exit Ubu.

MAMA UBU *(running after him)* Oh my God! Ubu,
get back here*! (picking up a half-unwrapped
burrito)* I'm gonna beat you with this!

UBU   *(offstage)* You know where you can stick
that burrito?!!

SCENE VI
The White House — the King's quarters.
KING WENCESLAS, surrounded
by OFFICERS; CAPTAIN BORDURE;
THE KING'S SONS. Then... Enter UBU.

UBU   Oh, Mr King, Sir! It wasn't me, it was
Mama Ubu and Bordure! I promise, I
promise.

KING   What have you been smoking?

CAPTAIN   Pay no attention to him, he was just…
              overindulging a little…at lunch with his
              celebrity friends.

KING   Oh, well, we all enjoy a little fun, every
              now and then.

UBU   Yeah, I'm having fun. Damn right I'm
              having fun! Like any other free American
              citizen enjoying this country!

KING   Ubu, I want to reward you for the
              services you've done for this country as
              Captain of the Dragoons, and today I want
              to make you Count of the Carolinas.

UBU   Oh, Mr King, how can I ever thank you?

KING   Don't thank me, Ubu – thank America.
              Now, that'll be all. And make sure to be
              fresh for tomorrow morning's big show of
              honours at the charity gala.

UBU   I'll be there. But please, sir, as a sign of my
              gratitude, accept this small kazoo.

He gives the King a kazoo.

KING   What do you want me to do with a kazoo?
Here, Buggerlaw, hold this,

BUGGERLAW This Ubu guy is an ass.

UBU   Sure, I'll get back to my work. (*He trips over while walking*) Oh my God! Assassins!
Terrorists! I've been shot!

KING   (*picking him up*) Ubu, are you alright?

UBU	Oh, yeah, you don't kill me that easy. One more thing, sir – what's my wife going to get, when I'm Count of the Carolinas?
KING	Oh, we can talk about that later.
UBU	Great, great. You get some rest, now.

Exit King.

> But don't think that picking me up off the floor is going to help you in the future, Mr King...

SCENE VII

Ubu Tower.

The Trumpeters; TRASH, TRITE and TRILLANY. UBU, MAMA UBU, CAPTAIN BORDURE, Soldiers and Hangers-On.

UBU	So! Everybody, it's about time we put the plan of action into place. Everybody gets to speak in turn, fair and equal. I'm going to begin, if you'll permit me.
CAPTAIN	Sure, go ahead.
UBU	Well, my friends, frankly, we need to poison the King. It's simple. I know about poison, and I know the best way to kill him

is to put arsenic in his lunch. When he
wants to eat it, he'll drop down dead, and
I'll be King.

All make noises of disgust and disappointment.

UBU   Please don't feel so pathetic and insecure –
I know you all know my ideas are the
best. Bordure, tell them.

CAPTAIN   Well, actually I think that sounds a bit of
a cowardly move, don't you? I think we
should rush in with swords and stab him,
right in front of everybody.

All cheer.

UBU   Oh, and what if he gets his own sword out?
And what about the Secret Service? I saw
yesterday that the King was wearing some
big, old iron boots – they'd hurt pretty bad
if he gave you a kicking. Jeez, you guys
are a bunch of losers. If only I'd thought
of it earlier, I would've denounced you to
the King for dragging me into this whole
mess. And I think I would've done pretty
well out of that.

MAMA UBU You are a selfish, orange, nightmare!

ALL　　　　　Boo to Ubu! Boo, boo, boo!

UBU　　　　Hey! Now, let's all calm down, OK? May I remind you that I'm the one holding the purse strings in this little escapade. If you're going to take the risk, I agree to take the chance on your method. By the way, Bordure, you'll be in charge of skewering the King's ass.

CAPTAIN　　Don't you think it'd be better if we all jumped him, together? We'd have a better chance of convincing the Secret Service not to put up a fight.

UBU　　　　OK then, good. Show how tough we are. I'm tasking you with stomping on his feet. He'll jump back in shock, and then I'll shout "FUCK YOU!" And on that signal, you'll pop him.

MAMA UBU Yeah, and as soon as he's dead I'll grab his badges and his rings.

CAPTAIN　　And then me and my men'll get the Royal Family!

UBU　　　　Yeah, get that annoying kid Buggerlaw.

Exit Ubu.

UBU   (*running back in*) Men, we have forgotten a
               totally indispensable part of this agree-
               ment! I want you all to swear an oath of
               loyalty to me...a kind of statement of
               allegiance, if you will...

CAPTAIN   Sure, but who's going to witness it? We
               don't have any priests or judges.

UBU   Oh, Mama Ubu can take that place.

ALL   Ubu forever!

UBU   Alright, Americans! Do you swear to kill
               the King with me, good and proper?

ALL   We swear! Long live Ubu!

END OF
ACT I

ACT II

THE WHITE HOUSE, King's quarters.
KING WENCESLAS, QUEEN ROSAMUND,
BOLESLAW, LAIDISLAW, BUGGERLAW.

KING   Young Buggerlaw, this morning you were exceedingly rude about Mr Ubu, a member of Congress and a businessman whose donations are extremely important to the administration's campaigns. For this reason, I forbid you to appear at the charity fund-raising gala today.

QUEEN   Oh, honey, but then you won't have all your family by your side – and you know the media will make up some rubbish about how we don't support you.

KING   Ma'am, I'm not even going to bother to reply to what you just said. You exhaust me sometimes.

BUGGERLAW I submit to my commanding officer's orders, Sir.

QUEEN   Anyway, honey, are you sure you really want to go to this gala anyway?

KING   And why not, ma'am?

QUEEN   But don't you remember what happened in my dream?

KING   What dream?

QUEEN   You know, the one where I saw you being beaten to death by a gang of masked men, and thrown in the fountains in the White House gardens, and an American golden eagle handing over the royal seal to him?

KING   No, I don't recall that at all. Handing the seal to who?

QUEEN   To Ubu!

KING   Oh, this is ridiculous! Mr Ubu is a great businessman, a gentleman and a well-known TV personality. Why, I believe he'd die in my service.

BUGGERLAW Huh – think again.

KING   Don't answer back to me, you young pup! And you, Ma'am, to prove to you the high regard in which I hold Mr Ubu, I'm going to go to tonight's gala just as I am now. With no Secret Service and no arms.

QUEEN   O fatal imprudence! I'll never see you alive again!!

KING   Come, Laidislaw; come, Boleslaw.

Exit King, Laidislaw and Boleslaw. Queen and Buggerlaw move to the window.

QUEEN AND BUGGERLAW God bless America!

QUEEN   Buggerlaw, let's go and watch the live broadcast of the gala on CNN. And pray for your father and your brothers!

SCENE II

The gala. A ballroom in The White House.
The Whole American Army. KING, BOLESLAW,
LAIDISLAW, UBU, CAPTAIN BORDURE and his
men, Trumpeters: TRASHTAG, TRITE, TRILLANY.

KING   Dear Ubu, I want you and your entourage
              to stand with me before I make my speech
              to the company.

UBU   *(to his men)* Attention, y'all. *(To King)*
              We're coming, Sir, we're coming.

Ubu's men surround the King.

KING   Ah! There's Angelina Jolie, here for the
              charity auction later. My, she's a fine-
              looking woman.

UBU   You think so? I think her *face* is a charity
              case. *(calling to Angelina)* Hey Angie, how
              long since you last shaved?

KING   I can't believe my ears. Are you disrespect-
              ing my guests, at a royal gala? And when
              did you last shave yourself!?

UBU   Now!

He stamps his foot.

KING   Get out!

UBU   FUCK YOU! To me, Americans!

CAPTAIN   Hurrah! Go get 'em!

All leap on the King. A small explosion is heard.

KING   Help! God! America! Terrorists! I'm dead!

BOLESLAW   *(to Laidislaw)* What's going on over there? Get your sword!

UBU   Ha ha ha! I have the Royal Seal! This is a truly tremendous moment in the history of American history. Get the sons, get the sons!

CAPTAIN   Kill the traitors!

The sons of the King flee. Men, Captain Bordure and Ubu follow them in pursuit.

SCENE III

The White House's TV room, where the QUEEN and BUGGERLAW have been watching a live broadcast of the gala.

QUEEN   At last, I'm beginning to feel a little better.

BUGGERLAW Yeah. I'm sure we have nothing to feel worried about.

Suddenly, an explosion is heard from outside. Both leap up and run to the window.

BUGGERLAW Huh? What am I seeing? My two brothers running across the grounds, and Ubu and his men chasing them with swords?

QUEEN   Oh my God! Oh my God, Buggerlaw, look! Trump's gang is gaining on them!

BUGGERLAW Look! The Whole American Army is following Ubu! This can't be happening! It's unprecedented – impossible! Where's our King?

QUEEN   Did you see that! They got Boleslaw!
             Beheaded him!

BUGGERLAW Oh! *(outside, Laidislaw turns to face the*
             onslaught) Save yourself!
             Hurrah, Laidislaw!

QUEEN   Oh! ...he's outnumbered. I can't look!

BUGGERLAW ...And it's all over. Bordure cut him in
             two like a piece of cherry pie.

QUEEN   Ah! Do you hear that, Buggerlaw? These
             terrorists are in the house now! Listen,
             they're on the stairs!

The clamour becomes louder and louder. The Queen
and Buggerlaw fall to their knees.

QUEEN & BUGGERLAW May God defend us!

BUGGERLAW Oh, this monster Ubu! And I thought
             he was just some upstart, white-trash
             moron in a wig! If I was face-to-face with
             him right now...

SCENE IV

The same. The door has been reinforced, with the TV and other furnishings piled against it, but is bulging dangerously with every fresh onslaught from outside. As we watch, UBU and his forces finally burst through, waving swords.

UBU   Hi, Buggerlaw. Hi, Queen. Now, look what you've made me do. You are very dishonest people. What am I supposed to do with you?

BUGGERLAW *(pulling out a gun)* God bless America! I'll defend my mother to the death! The first man to move, dies!

UBU   Ooh! Bordure, I'm frightened! Ickle Buggerlaw is waving his ickle weapon around... and you know what they say about men with small guns.

A soldier advances.

SOLDIER Drop the gun, son.

BUGGERLAW Hey, stop, you thug! Here's my answer to you –

He waves the gun and shoots the soldier.

QUEEN   Oh, good, Buggerlaw, good shot!

More soldiers begin slowly advancing towards Buggerlaw.

UBU   Now, Buggerlaw, I promise we won't hurt
             you. I promise.

BUGGERLAW You scrotum!

*He fires several more shots in the air, and then into the soldiers, who
are taken aback. Some clumsily attempt to draw their weapons, but*

each time, Buggerlaw gets there first, shooting them, then kicking their swords out of their hands. It is a massacre.

UBU   Oh, crap! Well, this isn't necessarily a disaster. In fact, I call this a success. We were hugely outnumbered. I never expected to win. We did great to get this far.

BUGGERLAW Mom, save yourself – get out through the secret passageway!

QUEEN   But you, my son, what are you going to do?

BUGGERLAW I'm right behind you.

UBU   Hey, will someone get that bitch? Just grab her by the pussy, or something? I'm going to get this pathetic little...

He marches towards Buggerlaw.

BUGGERLAW For my father and for America! Here's my revenge!

He drops his gun, lunges forward and seizes Ubu's scalp, peeling off the golden wig in one smooth motion. Then kicks him in the groin for good measure. Ubu falls on his face.

UBU   Howl, howl, howl!

BUGGERLAW I'm right behind you, Mom!

He disappears into the secret passageway.

SCENE V
A cave in the Rocky mountains.
BUGGERLAW enters, followed by
QUEEN ROSAMUND.

BUGGERLAW We're safe here, for now.

QUEEN   Yeah, I hope so. Oh, Buggerlaw, catch me!

She faints onto the snowy ground.

BUGGERLAW Huh? Mom, what's wrong?

QUEEN   I'm sick, honey. Believe me when I tell
               you I've no more than two hours to live!

BUGGERLAW Aw, I'm sure it's just a cold.

QUEEN   How can I live, after all we've seen
               today? The King murdered, our family
               torn apart, the noblest and ancientest blood
               in America, and we're forced to flee to the

mountains, treated like terrorists in our own country!

BUGGERLAW And by who, by God? By who! A vulgar tradesman! An upstart from who-knows-where – Queens – a vile misogynist, a warmonger, a bigot, a coward! And when I think that my father decorated him, and that the next day this villain had the audacity to raise arms against him!

QUEEN Oh, honey! When I think how happy we were before this awful Ubu arrived on the scene! Alas, how quickly life can be turned upside down...

BUGGERLAW Mom, we have to look to the future. Change only happens when individuals get involved, get engaged, and demand it themselves.

QUEEN I hope you succeed in your honourable task, my love. Alas for me, I won't see the happy day when you are restored to your rightful place in the annals of American history.

BUGGERLAW Huh? What are you saying? Your face is turning a funny colour – she's falling over! Mom! Won't somebody help us?! Oh God, I'm really all alone! Her heart's stopped beating. Dead! Another victim of Ubu. *(He hides his face in his hands and weeps.)* Oh, God! Isn't it sad, to be fourteen years old and already have a terrible vengeance to fulfil?

He falls to the ground and succumbs to his despair. At this point, the GHOSTS of Wenceslas, Boleslaw, Laidislaw and Rosamund enter the cave, accompanied by their ANCESTORS. The most ancient ANCESTOR approaches the prone figure of Buggerlaw, and gently rouses him.

BUGGERLAW What do I see here? Mom, Dad? But transparent?

GHOST   Listen, Buggerlaw. During life, I was known by the name George Washington.

I was the first King of America, and your distant relation...some kind of uncle, I think, several times removed. I am here to give you the means to fulfil your destiny! *(He hands Buggerlaw a huge sword.)* This sword that I give you shall never have rest until you take your rightful seat in the Oval Office.

With that, the Ghosts vanish. Buggerlaw is left alone, in an attitude of extreme exhaustion.

SCENE VI
The White House, Royal quarters.
UBU, MAMA UBU, CAPTAIN BORDURE.

UBU   No, I don't want to! Are you trying to ruin me?

CAPTAIN   But, Sir, don't you want this to be the best-attended inauguration of all time?

MAMA UBU   If you don't give out free food and throw money around, you'll be headed right back where you started from – or worse.

UBU   Free food, fine! Money, no! Kill a few old cows, that'll be enough for some crappy hamburgers to feed the trash in this city.

MAMA UBU Trash, yourself! Where am I going to find these old cows?

UBU For the last time, I want to get *rich*. I don't want to spend a penny.

MAMA UBU Ugh, when you have the richest country in the world under your thumb...

CAPTAIN Yeah, and I happen to know that in the cellar there's tons of gold! We could give that out?

UBU What! You moron, if you dare do such a thing!

BORDURE But, Sir, if you don't give the people a break, they won't pay their taxes.

UBU Is this true?

MAMA UBU Yes, yes!

UBU Oh, well then, I consent to everything. Give out three million dollars, have five hundred cows and sheep killed for beefburgers and sheepburgers...and make sure you save some of those burgers for me.

SCENE VII

A raised stage at a rally in a large park.
UBU, now King; MAMA UBU; CAPTAIN
BORDURE; Flunkies carrying food.

PEOPLE: The King! U-S-A! U-S-A!

UBU   *(throwing money)* Wait. No, that's for you,
       honey, for your beautiful pair of – eyes!
       You know, it doesn't amuse me any, giving
       you this money. But, you know, my wife
       told me to – and you know what women
       are like at their time of the month! You
       better promise to pay your taxes! Heh, heh.

ALL   Yes, yes! U-S-A! U-S-A!

CAPTAIN Look, Madame Ubu, how they fight for
       the last pennies. Quite a disgusting
       spectacle.

MAMA UBU It's true, it's horrible. Pah! Look, there,
       one of them is already bleeding.

UBU   What a wonderful sight! Chaos, chaos
       everywhere! Bring out more chests of
       money.

CAPTAIN We should start a race for the money...

UBU   How about we have a race? No need to congratulate me on the idea, I only have great ideas. *(To the people.)* My friends, you see this chest of money? It contains three million dollars! That's more than you've ever seen in your life! It's a tremendous, terrific amount of money. And I'm going to give this to you – yes, *you* – if you are the winner of the Inaugural Annual Ub-a-thon. I'm not saying it's going to be easy. But if you don't take part, you'll be a loser before you've even started. And if you do take part, you'll be rewarded with an extra dollop of ketchup on the next Ubu Certified Beefburger you buy today – free!

ALL   Yes! God bless Ubu! God bless the King! We never had any fun like this with Wenceslas.

UBU   *(whispering to Mama Ubu, joyfully)* Listen! They love me!

The people arrange themselves along a starting line

UBU   One, two, three – ready?

ALL   Yes!

UBU   Go!

They run into the wings.
Cries and crashing noises from offstage.

CAPTAIN   They're approaching
            the finish line!

UBU   Hey! That guy in front – he's losing
            ground!

MAMA UBU No, he's catching up now!

UBU   He's bound to win! It's a foregone
            conclusion.

MAMA UBU I'm sure of it!

UBU   He'll definitely win. I'm an expert in
            predicting winners. All the signs point to
            him winning.

CAPTAIN   Yeah! Oh! Yeah! He's lost, he's lost! It's all
            over!

The competitor who was in second place pulls ahead, revealing
that he has been holding back. To the surprise and consternation
of spectators and photographers, he crosses the finish line before the
frontrunner.

ALL   Go, Don! Go, Don!

DONALD THE RUNNER Sir, I don't know how I
can begin to thank you.

UBU   Son, you don't need to begin right now.
                   You just pick up that chest and take it home
                   – and, the rest of you, share the second
                   chest amongst yourselves! You deserve it!
                   God rewards hardworking people.

ALL   Go Don! Go, Ubu! U-S-A!

UBU   And you, my friends and family, how about
                   we get something to eat? It's about time!
                   Throw open the doors of the White
                   House!

ALL   Open the doors! Give me a U-B-U! Make
                   America great again!

*They enter the White House. We hear orgiastic noises, sounds of
revelry and bacchanalia, as the sun sets. The curtain falls.*

*END OF
ACT II*

ACT III

SCENE I

The White House, Royal quarters.
UBU, MAMA UBU

UBU   Well, in the end, your life isn't measured
      by what you undertake; it's measured
      by what you accomplish. And look, I'm
      King of the United States of America. I've
      already given myself indigestion with
      the number of steaks I've eaten, and right
      this minute some flunky is combing
      my new state wig. Good? Good? That's
      good.

MAMA UBU New wig? And what's that made of?
      Being made King is all very well, but we
      have to *look* as though we're economising.

UBU   Ma'am, the State Wig is the very best
      money can buy. It's made of golden wires,
      hand-stitched by Ralph Lauren's top
      couturiers onto a silk-and-silicon cap.

MAMA UBU Yeah, very nice. But you'd better not get
      too big for your boots.

UBU   You'd better watch you don't get too
      big for your boobs. I could move on to
      Wife No. 4 at any moment.

MAMA UBU Have you reached out to the Duke of
California yet? We owe him a lot.

UBU Who?

MAMA UBU Captain Bordure!

UBU Don't talk to me about that moron. You
know, we don't need him. We don't
need him, any more. He can eat my shorts;
he's not getting California!

MAMA UBU You should be ashamed of yourself!
He'll turn against you.

UBU You know, I'm not scared. I feel sorry for
him. I feel sorry for this little man. He
worries me about as much as that kid
Buggerlaw does.

MAMA UBU Huh! You think we're done with
Buggerlaw?

UBU You bet your ass I do. What can a spotty
teenager do to me, Ubu? This administration is the cleverest and the best
America has ever had.

MAMA UBU Ubu, you should listen to me. We should
try to get Buggerlaw on our side.

UBU   You have got to be joking. Is she joking? I don't think that's gonna happen.

MAMA UBU Think of saving your own ass, Ubu!

UBU   Well, your ass will be in the shit along with mine!

MAMA UBU Listen, please, just one more time... I'm sure that young Buggerlaw will be dangerous to us – after all, he has justice on his side...

UBU   What! I'm tough, I'm smart and I'm the best businessman in America – don't I have just as much right to be King as him? I think I have more right. You know what, you are unacceptable! I'm gonna show you how wrong you are!

He leaps up and chases Mama Ubu offstage.

SCENE II

The White House, The Oval Office.
UBU, MAMA UBU, Officers and
Soldiers, Trumpeters TRASHTAG, TRITE, and
TRILLANY. POLITICIANS in chains. Businessmen,
Magistrates, Clerks.

UBU   Bring the Royal Trunk and the Royal Golf
               Club and the Royal Sword and the Royal
               Book! And then – bring in the Politicians!

The chained politicians shuffle on stage, pushed by clerks.

MAMA UBU Jeez, Ubu, show a little moderation.

UBU   Today, ladies and gentlemen, I've the
               pleasure of announcing that
               I'm gonna enrich the country. Yes, I
               know a lot about making money. Look at
               me. Just look at me. And something has
               to be done with this country. And we
               have to be tough about it. And so, I'm
               gonna kill all the politicians and confiscate
               their belongings.

POLITICIANS No! Horror! Help us!

UBU   Bring me the first politician! And pass me
               the Royal Golf Club, would you, honey?
               Those who have to die, will go through the
               trapdoor. They'll fall into the White
               House basement, and then they'll be taken
               to the dungeons below, where their brains
               will be removed by the Destroying
               Machine – a very up-to-date piece
               of machinery, that – cutting edge.
               Let's hear it for American technology!

(To the first Politician) Who are you then, you with the little hands?

POLITICIAN I'm from Florida.

UBU   And what are your revenues?

POLITICIAN Three million dollars a year.

UBU   Trapdoor!

Ubu hits the Politician with the Golf Club, and the Politician falls into the trapdoor.

MAMA UBU Ferocious!

UBU   Second Politician! You, the sly-looking
                    one. Who are you? *(The Second Politician
                    does not reply.)* Answer me, you liar!

SECOND POLITICIAN I'm a senator for Texas.

UBU   Good, good – the oil state! Do I need to
                    ask anything else? Through the trapdoor!
                    *(He hits him. Politician falls to his knees,
                    and tumbles through the trapdoor.)* Third
                    Politician! You look pretty low energy.
                    How did you ever get to be a politician?
                    Hey, can you imagine this guy ever
                    becoming King?

THIRD POLITICIAN I'm called Jeb. And I belong to
                    one of America's greatest political
                    dynasties, I'll have you know!

UBU   Excellent, excellent! Any more to say?

THIRD POLITICIAN Uh…no.

UBU   Through the trapdoor, then. Fourth
                    Politician, who are you?

FOURTH POLITICIAN I'm from Vermont.

UBU   What are your revenues?

FOURTH POLITICIAN I give most of mine away to
the poor.

UBU   Well, for using such foul language, you can
go through the trapdoor too. Next! Who
you, lady?

FIFTH POLITICIAN I was high up in Wenceslas'
administration. You aren't going to get
away with lying to the people, Ubu.

UBU   You know, Wenceslas lied to the people a
lot. A lot. I mean, did *you* ever see his birth
certificate?

FIFTH POLITICIAN What nonsense are you talking
about?

UBU   Enough! Trapdoor! What are you snivelling
about, Mama?

MAMA UBU You're too harsh, Ubu!

UBU   Whatever! I'm just trying to make a living.
A man's gotta look after himself. Now, I'm
going to have them read out a list of MY
possessions and MY titles.

TRASHTAG THE TRUMPETER Principality of
El Paso, Grand-Duchy of Detroit, Duchy

of Des Moines, Earldom of Illinois,
Palatinate of Palm Springs, Margraviate
of Manhattan Island.

UBU   Go on!

TRASH   That's it.

UBU   How is that it? Oh, well then, let's get on
with the Politicians, and seeing as it's taking
so long to get rich in this country, I'll just
execute them all and confiscate all their
goods. C'mon, stick 'em in.

*Clerks and Trumpeters funnel the Politicians through the trapdoor,
as quickly as they can. Some politicians, being on the chubby side,
become stuck.*

UBU   Hurry up, you assholes! I want to go and
               make some laws!

CLERKS/TRUMPETERS This we gotta see!

*They stuff the remaining Politicians through the trapdoors as fast
as they can.*

UBU   Okay, so first of all I'm gonna reform
               immigration. People, there is something
               seriously wrong with our immigration
               system. Then I'll proceed with economical
               system.

MAGISTRATES We oppose any and all reforms to the
               entry requirements into the United States.

UBU   Fuck. Right. From now on, magistrates
               aren't going to be paid by the public sector.

MAGISTRATES What? How are we going to live?
               We'll be poor!

UBU   Oh, you can keep any fines you impose,
               and you can confiscate the possessions of
               those you condemn to death.

A MAGISTRATE Horror!

SECOND MAGISTRATE Infamy!

THIRD MAGISTRATE Scandal!

FOURTH MAGISTRATE Indignity!

MAGISTRATES We refuse to work under such
conditions.

UBU   Fuck you all! Through the trapdoor with
the magistrates!

*The puny Magistrates struggle in vain against the strong arms of
the Trumpeters and Clerks.*

MAMA UBU Oh my Lord! Ubu, what are you doing?
Who's gonna maintain justice in our
country, now?

UBU   Shut your mouth! I will. You'll see, it'll all
be tremendous. Terrific.

MAMA UBU Yeah, sure – it'll be chaos.

UBU   Again – shut your mouth, you brainless
whore. Now, gentlemen, let's proceed with
the economic situation.

BUSINESSMEN Nothing needs changing. Everything
works fine.

UBU   Yeah, but I wanna change everything. First
of all, of course, I want half of all taxes to

come straight to the pockets of Ubu
Incorporated.

BUSINESSMEN Not possible. We know how
       government works – trust us to run
       everything, like we always do.

UBU   Gentlemen, let's bring in a new tax of 10%
       of property, another on trade and industry,
       a third on marriage, and a fourth on death.
       Of $50 each. How's that deal for you?

FIRST BUSINESSMAN But Sir, that's absurd.

SECOND BUSINESSMAN Mr King, it's
       ridiculous, if you'll pardon
       my French.

THIRD BUSINESSMAN That's not a
       deal – you've only just
       thought of that now!

UBU   You arguing with me?
       I've got a louder voice and
       a bigger advertising budget
       than you! I can make
       whatever shit I do smell
       sweet! Through the trapdoor!

*Trumpeters seize the Businessmen and drag them
over to the trapdoor.*

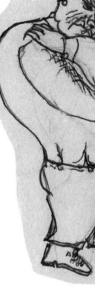

MAMA UBU   Oh my God, Ubu, you're even worse at being King than I imagined...you've silenced everyone who dares speak against you!

UBU   Fuck the haters!

MAMA UBU   No more justice, no more business!

UBU   Don't worry, sweetheart. I'll go on a nationwide tour, rallies in every major city, to make sure everybody loves me and I can collect all the taxes I'm owed.

SCENE III

A town hall in a small town, somewhere in Middle America. A group of poverty-stricken TOWNSPEOPLE is assembled.

PEASANT   *(entering, brandishing a newspaper)* Guys, have you heard the news! The King and his sons are dead, and most of Congress – all except Young Buggerlaw and his Mom, who've escaped to Alaska! And to top it all, the new King is Ubu!

ANOTHER   Yeah, I heard more! I saw a video online of the bodies of 300 politicians and 500 magistrates that they've had murdered! They're gonna triple our taxes, and Ubu's gonna come to collect them himself!

ALL   Oh my God! Alas! What will become of
            us? Ubu is evil! And his wife is even worse,
            look at those slutty clothes she wears.

PEASANT   Listen! Is that someone at the door?

A VOICE   *(from outside)* Chaos and bloodshed! Open
            up, by order of the King! Open, you
            shitfaces, you assholes, you cheapskates –
            I want my money!

*The door is broken open. UBU forces his way through, followed
by the Whole American Army, TRUMPETERS and Money-
Grubbers.*

SCENE IV
The same.

UBU   Which of you is the oldest, here? *(A peasant
            steps forward.)* Eew. What do they call you?

PEASANT   Abraham.

UBU   Cool. Well then, Abe, listen up, or these
            gentlemen here will cut your ears off. Heh,
            heh, heh! You listening?

PEASANT   Sir, you ain't said much yet.

UBU   That's a lie, from the liberal press! I've been
             talking for over an hour! Am I
             preaching in a desert, here? Does
             nobody ever listen to the truth? (*Sighs.*) I'm
             beginning to understand how Jesus felt.

PEASANT   Sir, that thought sure didn't occur to me.

UBU   Well, I've come to direct you to produce
             all your finances and records of what you
             possess, immediately. Or else you'll be
             massacred. *(To his followers and Money-
             Grubbers.)* Let's go, gentlemen. Get in the
             Money Wagons.

*Enter the 'Money Wagons' – flashy limousines emblazoned with
dollar signs, reminders to pay taxes, and Ubu's face.*

PEASANT   Sir, we're down on the census for only
             $1520, which we paid six weeks ago come
             Sunday.

UBU   That's possible. In fact, it's extremely
             possible. However, things change rapidly
             with the global state of affairs, you know,
             and I've already told you in my press
             releases, you know, that you'll have to pay
             all existing taxes twice, and three times
             subsequently if you can't pay on time. With
             this system, I'll make my fortune quickly –
             then I'll retire and let them starve!

PEASANTS   Mr King, sir, have pity on us! We are only
             poor citizens, but we're free Americans.

UBU   Who gives a shit? I'm tough. That's why
             I'm a success, and you're poor. Go eat each
             other.

PEASANTS   We can't afford to pay any more.

UBU   Pay! Or I'll fill my pockets with your heads,
             sliced off of your bodies! Goddammit,
             aren't I the King? You should be glad to pay
             me taxes – I am America!

PEASANTS   So it comes to this! To arms! Down with
             King Ubu! Long live Buggerlaw, by the
             grace of God and the American people,
             King of the United States, and rightful heir
             to Good King Wenceslas!

UBU   Well, fine, if that's what you want. Soldiers,
             do what you must.

*He wanders offstage as the fighting begins. The town hall is
quickly destroyed – peasants and soldiers using the flag of the
Confederate flag, the podium and microphone, and the framed
Declaration of Independence to beat each other. At last, the army
has massacred the townspeople – the sole survivor being tough old
ABRAHAM, who flees, defeated. UBU strolls back on, and takes
a seat to count his money.*

SCENE V

A dungeon in Alcatraz, Guantanamo, or somewhere.
CAPTAIN BORDURE chained to the wall. Enter UBU.

UBU   Oh, hey – didn't see you there!
             Well, *(indicates Captain Bordure's chains.)* I

guess this is how it's gonna be from now
on. You wanted me to pay you, or
something, so you thought you'd kick up a
fuss, and now look what you've got out
of it. Well, that's to be expected! It was well
done by me to lock you up. Yes, well done
indeed. It's what you deserve, you son of a
bitch.

CAPTAIN   Take care, Ubu. In the five days you've
           ruled this country, you've committed
           enough crimes to damn all the Founding
           Fathers! The blood of the politicians and
           the Royal Family cries out for vengeance,
           and their cries will be heard!!

UBU   You're talking about some heavy stuff
           there. I have no doubt, no doubt at all,
           that if you were to escape it could cause
           some very big problems for America. But I
           don't think that these guards have ever
           let go of any of the fine people entrusted to
           their care... Anyway, good night! I hope
           you sleep well. Though I hear the rats here
           do a very pretty tap dance at night, which I
           do hope doesn't keep you awake...

He leaves. Jailers enter to lock all the doors.

SCENE VI
THE KREMLIN, MOSCOW
TSAR VLADIMIR; his court; CAPTAIN BORDURE.

TSAR   So, Captain Bordure, the infamous
           adventurer, who had a hand in the plot to
           murder my own cousin, Wenceslas!

CAPTAIN   Mr Tsar, Sir, I mostly humbly beg your
          pardon. I was forced into it in spite of my
          own doubts, by that terrible Ubu.

TSAR   Oh, you bare-faced liar! Well, what do
          you think you'll get out of Russia?

CAPTAIN   Ubu imprisoned me, on a trumped-
          up charge of conspiracy. I managed to
          escape, and journeyed on a highly
          convoluted route by plane, train and
          automobile in order to reach you, and
          implore your Graciousness to have mercy
          upon me.

TSAR   What makes you think I can trust you?

CAPTAIN   I'll give you my sword and a detailed
           account of the American military's location
           and taskforce.

TSAR   I'll take the sword – but you can stick the
           account up your ass. I don't want to owe
           my triumphs to treason.

CAPTAIN   One of Wenceslas' sons, Young Buggerlaw,
           lives yet – I would do anything to restore
           him to his rightful place in the Oval Office.

TSAR   What rank were you in the army?

CAPTAIN   I commanded the 5th Regiment of the
           Washington Dragoons, and also Ubu's
           personal guards.

TSAR   Cool. I'll make you Lieutenant of the
           10th Cossack Regiment, and watch out you
           don't betray the trust I'm putting in you. If
           you fight well, you'll be well rewarded.

CAPTAIN   I do not lack courage, Sire.

TSAR   Yeah, whatever. Now get out of my sight!

Exit Captain Bordure.

SCENE VII

The Oval Office, during a meeting.
UBU, MAMA UBU, Business Advisors.

UBU   Gentlemen, this meeting is now in session
       and can proceed. All you have to do is
       sit down and shut up. First of all, we're
       gonna set out a new budget, then we'll talk
       about a little system I just thought up,
       to ensure good weather forever, and
       for bringing rain when we want it.

AN ADVISOR Sounds great, Sir!

MAMA UBU He's a coked-up, rambling moron.

UBU   Ma'am, would you do us all the kindness
       of keeping your hormones to yourself?
       Thanks. Now, gentlemen, I have been
       informed by leading experts that the
       finances are going better than they ever
       have before. You know those rich old ladies
       who dress their dogs up in woolly coats?
       Yeah, well a LOT of those dogs have
       been seen about recently. Which can
       only mean that we have a LOT of rich old
       ladies, am I right? These bastard dognappers
       are going crazy for 'em! People are literally
       going mad under the weight of how much
       money is coming in.

ANOTHER ADVISOR And the new taxes, Sir, how
     are they going?

MAMA UBU A total fuck-up. The new tax on marriage
     has made $11 so far, so Ubu's been going
     around trying to force people to get
     married.

UBU   Holy shit, woman! What are you, a
     mathematician or an economist or
     something? *(He howls with insane laughter.)*
     You're driving me crazy – you're making
     me real mad! Holy fucking Ubu Tower...!

Enter a Messenger

     Oh, good, great – so what do you want? Get
     out, asshole, or I'll fire your ass! Literally!
     Ha, ha, ha!

Messenger flees.

MAMA UBU Ah! He dropped this letter as he ran away.

UBU   Read it out. I can read, of course, I just
     don't want to right now. Hurry up! It looks
     like it's from Bordure.

MAMA UBU For once, you're right. He says that the
     Tsar has welcomed him in Russia, that he's

planning to invade the States and
install Buggerlaw as King, and that
you're gonna be hung out to dry.

UBU   Ha, ha, ha! I'm so scared! Ha, ha! I
           think I'll die! Oh no, what'm I gonna
           do? This dumb little man is gonna kill
           me! The holy fucking Virgin and all the
           saints protect me! Ha, ha!

Pause. Sudden terror.

           Protect me! I'm being threatened by
           foreign powers!

*He bursts into tears and falls to grasp the feet of Mama Ubu,
sobbing and howling.*

MAMA UBU There's only one way out of this mess.

UBU   Oh, honey, what is it?

MAMA UBU War!!!

ALL   Praise the Lord! That's the right path to
           take!

UBU   Oh yeah, and now I'll suffer even more.

FIRST ADVISOR Let's run to organise the army!

SECOND ADVISOR And to get rations together!

THIRD ADVISOR And to prepare artillery and
defence!

FOURTH ADVISOR And to raise money for the
troops!

UBU   Hold it right there! I'll kill anyone who
moves before I'm done! I wanna make very
clear that I won't be spending any money. I
used to get paid during wars, when I was
selling things to the army...and now I
have to fund them at my own expense. And
I don't like that. I don't like it at all. You
make war, if you're so 'mad' – just don't
expect me to shell out one single cent!

ALL   Hurrah for war!

SCENE VIII

*An encampment on the coast of America. The Whole
American Army preparing to set sail.
UBU, surrounded by Louis Vuitton suitcases and fripperies,
MAMA UBU, Soldiers, Minions, Horse.*

SOLDIERS AND MINIONS God bless America! God
bless King Ubu! Make America great again!

UBU   Mama Ubu, give me my special five-iron
                  club with the sword concealed inside it,
                  and my Tommy Hilfiger bulletproof vest.
                  Jeez, I'll be so weighed down I won't be
                  able to run away.

MAMA UBU Eew, you're such a scaredy-cat.

UBU   It's always the shitty sword that breaks at
                  the last minute, or the crappy shield that
                  doesn't hold up… *(stamps his foot)* Aw man,
                  I'll never be ready, and the Russians are
                  getting close and they're going to kill me…

A SOLDIER Mr King Sir, you're losing it.

UBU   Will you just fuck off, you little twerp!
                  I'm gonna kill you with these… *(casts
                  around himself looking for a suitable weapon)*
                  …nail scissors.

MAMA UBU *(to audience)* Wow, don't you think he
                  looks good with his helmet and his
                  breastplate on? One is put in mind of an
                  armed pumpkin.

UBU   Okay, gentlemen, I'm now gonna get
                  on my horse. I want the best horse you've
                  got!

MAMA UBU   Ubu, the horse won't be able to carry
            your weight – your orders were to give
            the horses' food to the low-ranking
            soldiers. The horses haven't been
            fed for five days.

UBU   Eh, now you tell me! I pay twelve cents
            every day for this nag and I can't even
            ride it. Holy shit, are you kidding me?
            I ain't putting up with this! I don't pay for
            something I can't ride! *(Mama Ubu blushes
            and lowers her gaze.)* Well then, get
            moving! I ain't gonna walk!

An enormous horse is brought onstage.

UBU   Okay, cool, I'll ride that.
            Oh, it's big. *(he clambers
            awkwardly on.)* Oh, heck.
            Oh, I'm gonna fall!

The horse slowly walks offstage.
Ubu is left behind.

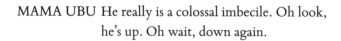

            Hey, stop! Stop that horse!
            My God, I fell off!

MAMA UBU   He really is a colossal imbecile. Oh look,
            he's up. Oh wait, down again.

UBU   Jesus Christ, I'm half-dead! Well, I didn't
               want a horse anyhow. It all went much
               better than expected. I only wanted to
               ride it for a second. It was a tremendous
               success! Now, let's go to war and kill
               everybody! Russia, China, Korea, the
               British Isles – make America great
               again!

MAMA UBU   Good luck, honey.

UBU   I forgot to mention that I'm making
               you Acting King in my absence. But
               I'm taking the accounts with me. Tough
               shit for you if you wanted to make
               money out of this whole 'being married
               to the King' thing. I'll leave Trumpeter
               Trashtag with you. Bye now.

MAMA UBU   Adieu, Ubu. Make sure you kill the Tsar
               good and proper.

UBU   For sure! Twisting of the nose and teeth,
               full tongue extraction and insertion of
               splinters beneath the nails.

The army, led by Ubu, moves off to the sound of fanfares.

MAMA UBU *(alone)* Now that stooge is gone, I can finally get to work. Get Buggerlaw killed, and then find Wenceslas' hidden treasure...!

END OF
ACT III

ACT IV

SCENE I

A dank crypt: the ancient burial ground of American royalty.
MAMA UBU.

MAMA UBU Okay, so where in God's name is this treasure? None of these asshole tiles sound hollow, and I've tapped every damn one! Thirteen tiles along from the tomb of Laidislaw the Great, going along the wall – nothing! No, wait, what's that? To work, Mama Ubu! C'mon, dig deeper, deeper, there must be something they've kept hidden...now what if I use my dagger...*et voila*! Here's the gold buried alongside the bones of the Kings! Ha, ha, I can't believe how clever I am!

She suddenly stops, startled, having heard something inaudible to the audience.

> What was that? Are there those yet
> living, in these ancient vaults? No, that
> can't be true. It was definitely nothing.
> I made it up. C'mon, Mama, make sure you
> get it all. This gold will look better in the
> light of day than now, surrounded by a
> bunch of dead guys. Now, push the tile
> back...good! Huh – still that noise in my
> ears? Well, that's weird. Obviously, being
> in this creepy place is making me freaky; I
> better take a break. I'll come back for the
> rest of the gold later.

A VOICE   *(from the tomb of George Washington)*
            Mama Ubu, you shall return – nevermore!

Mama Ubu jumps up, affronted, gathers up the gold and stalks out.

SCENE II
Times Square
BUGGERLAW and his Guerillas, People, Soldiers.

BUGGERLAW To arms, my friends! To the memory of
            the glorious Wenceslas! That old ball-
            ache Ubu has left the country, and only
            that witch of a wife of his stands in our

way. I offer my services for America, to
march at the head of your army and re-
establish the race of my forefathers
as the leaders of the American people.

ALL   Hooray!

BUGGERLAW And, we'll be suspending all
             of Ubu's taxes until further notice!

ALL   Hooray! Long live Buggerlaw! To arms!
             Let's attack the White House!

BUGGERLAW Oh, shit! Here comes the Royal cavalcade,
             with Mama Ubu and her guards!

MAMA UBU *(leaning out of a limo)*: What's going on
             over here? Oh my God! It's Buggerlaw!

The crowd begins to throw stones at the Secret Service's cavalcade.

FIRST GUARD Hey, they smashed the window of
             my limo!

SECOND GUARD Ouch, something hit me!

THIRD GUARD Holy crap, I'm dead!

BUGGERLAW Throw stones, Americans!

TRUMPETER TRASHTAG And so, the final conflict
has begun...

He unsheathes his sword, and begins massacring whole swathes of civilians.

BUGGERLAW *(to a close comrade)* Leave this one for me.

Buggerlaw and Trashtag fight.

TRASHTAG I am slain!

BUGGERLAW Victory, my friends! And now for
Mama Ubu!

The sound of Trumpets.

BUGGERLAW That must be the Politicians being set
free. Quick, catch her before she escapes in
the chaos!

ALL   She won't leave here except in a box!

Mama Ubu flees, pursued by the entire American populace. Shots, and a final hail of stones.

SCENE III

The American army on the march in Ukraine.
Ubu has made his camp inside a small barn on top of a hill.
UBU, TRITE, TRILLANY, Soldiers, GENERAL.

UBU   Jesus, Mary and fucking Jehoshaphat!
                  We're going to die of fatigue before we ever
                  reach the Russians! Hey you, do your
                  King the kindness of carrying our
                  moneybox, and you, carry our golf clubs.
                  Careful! And can some nice female soldier
                  come and make the King's bed, maybe pee
                  a little on it, too?

The soldiers obey.

TRITE   Hey, Mr King! Don't you think it's funny
                  that the Russians haven't shown up yet?

UBU   It's regrettable that our current financial
                  situation no longer permits there to be a
                  car suitable for our size and status. For
                  fear of causing irreparable damage to our
                  nag, we made the journey to Russia
                  on foot, leading the horse by the bridle.
                  However, on our triumphant re-entry into
                  the United States, we imagine, we'll build a
                  car – and nobody builds cars better than
                  me, believe me – that can transport
                  the whole army! And we'll build it very
                  inexpensively. Mark my words.

TRILLANY   Hey, sir, look – there goes the General.
           He's going pretty fast in the opposite
           direction to Russia.

UBU   Hey you! What's up with you?

GENERAL   All is lost. Sir, the Americans are
           revolting. Trashtag is dead and Mama Ubu
           has fled to the mountains.

UBU   Fuck! Does it never end? And who's
           leading them? Buggerlaw, I'll bet my ass.
           And where do you think you're going?

GENERAL   Washington, Sir.

UBU   You little twerp, if you think I'm gonna
           swallow this crock of shit and make the
           whole army turn around again, you can
           have another think coming! Get back
           to your post. The Russians aren't far off,
           and we're gonna throw them everything
           we've got.

GENERAL   Sir, don't you see the Russian encampment
           on the plain?!

UBU   Holy crap, he's right! There they are! Oh,
           now I'm really fucked! We're on a height
           and visible on all sides!

THE ARMY The Russians! The enemy!

UBU   Alright, gentlemen, take your positions for
             battle. We'll hold the high ground –
             whatever you do, don't be tricked into
             moving onto the plain. I'll be camped in
             the middle, at the top of the hill, and I
             want you to surround me with no gaps in
             my defences. I recommend you check your
             weapons are fully loaded, and make sure
             you don't waste shot. Eight bullets can kill
             eight Russians, and every one killed is
             one less off my back. We'll send the foot
             soldiers to the bottom of the hill to receive
             the Russian advance and kill the first few
             of 'em, the cavalry behind them to throw
             the enemy into a real confusion, and the
             artillery around this barn, here, to fire into
             the fray. As for my guard, we'll stay inside
             the barn and set up defences at the
             windows, bar the door and if anyone tries
             to enter, woe betide them – they're fucked!

OFFICERS   Your orders will be carried out, Mr King,
             sir.

UBU   Cool, very good, and then we'll win. I'm
             good with war. I know a lot about war.
             America needs strong leadership, and I'm
             the strongest. What time is it?

ALFRED JARRY / ROSANNA HILDYARD

UBU   Time for a snack before the Russians get
           here. They won't arrive before midday. Tell
           the soldiers, General, to get ready and get
           'em to sing the new national anthem 'The
           Golden-Headed Hero'.

Exit General.

SOLDIERS AND MINIONS Long live Ubu! Make
           America great again!

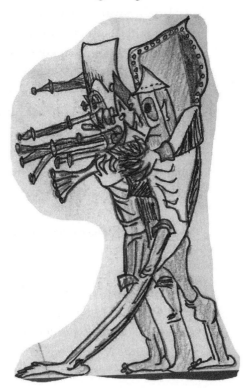

UBU   Oh, brave men, I love it when you say such
       things. God bless y'all. *(A Russian bullet
       strikes the roof of the barn.)* Aiee! I'm scared!
       I'm hit! I'm dying! Wait, no, I'm fine.
       Don't panic; you can stop panicking.

SCENE IV

*The same. A Soldier, UBU, GENERAL.
Then, The Whole Russian Army.*

SOLDIER   *(arriving)* Mr King, the Russians have
          arrived!

UBU   Yeah? And what do you want me to do
          about it? It's not me you've gotta speak to!
          Prepare for combat yourselves!

A second bullet zings into the barn.

GENERAL   A second bullet!

UBU   Oh my God! I can't stand this any longer.
          It's raining fire and bullets out there, and
          we could be endangering my precious
          safety! Let's get out of here!

*Ubu, assorted Minions, Ubu's Guard and the General creep out
of the barn and clamber downhill. The armies have just begun to
engage. Our little gang disappears amid gunsmoke and explosions.*

RUSSIAN   *(firing a machine gun)* For God and the Tsar!

GENERAL   Ah! I'm hit!

UBU   Shit! To me, guards! Hey, you Russian
            asshole, if you hit me I'm going to hit you
            back, harder, you hear me? Fuck you! And
            your stupid Russian gun that doesn't work,
            ha, ha!

RUSSIAN   Ha! Get a taste of this!

He shoots at Ubu.

UBU   Ow! Ooh! I'm hurt, I'm pierced right
            through, I'm killed! I can see the light at
            the end of the tunnel! I'm buried! Except
            that he missed! Ha, now I have you! *(He
            shoots the Russian.)* I got him! Now we've
            started something.

GENERAL   Advance! Push forward, men! Across the
            river! Victory is ours!

UBU   Think so? I can see more bastard Russians
            than Americans.

RUSSIAN ARMY Hurrah! Make way for the Tsar!

*Enter the Tsar Vladimir, with Captain Bordure at his side in
disguise.*

AMERICAN SOLDIER Oh my God! It's every man for himself now – here comes the Tsar!!!

SECOND SOLDIER Oh my God! He's crossing the river towards our camp!

THIRD SOLDIER Bang! Bang! Do you see that? Four Americans knocked unconscious by that big bastard next to him!

CAPTAIN Ha! Had enough, have you? Already? Yeah, get your fill of this, sir! *(he moves through the soldiers, knocking them down easily.)* C'mon, men, get the rest of 'em!

The Russians begin massacring the fleeing Americans.

UBU Advance, my friends, advance, for Chrissake! Get that big asshole! Victory is ours! Make America great again!

ALL Advance! For Ubu! Get the bastards!

CAPTAIN Jeez – I'm hit!

UBU *(recognising him)* Oh Lord – it's Captain Bordure! So, my old friend, it's come to this! I am really glad to see you. No, really, so glad. I'm so glad to see you, because I'm gonna roast you and eat you with cranberry sauce for dinner tonight. Mr Secretary, will you turn the oven on? *(a loud bang goes off.)* Oh my God! Terrorists, again! Help! I'm dying, I'm dying. Oh God. This whole thing was rigged from the start.

CAPTAIN   That was a cap pistol.

UBU   Oh, so you're mocking me now? You trying to take the piss? Yeah? I'll show you!

Surprisingly nimble, he rushes at Captain Bordure with his golf club raised high, and smashes it into Bordure's head, killing him outright.

GENERAL   Mr King, we're pressing our advantage to move forward on all fronts!

UBU   Sure, sure, whatever you want...I'm exhausted with my own heroism. *(Sits down with a bump.)* Ow! My balls!

GENERAL   Hey, sir, you should just go and grab the Tsar's as replacement.

UBU   Huh. You know, that's not actually a bad idea. *(leaping to his feet)* C'mon! My noble golf iron will aid me and share with me the honour of insulting, embarrassing, and destroying the Tsar of Russia! Guards, advance!

He runs towards the Tsar.

A RUSSIAN OFFICER Your Majesty! Watch out!

UBU   Shut up! And take that! Oh! Ow! Fuck!
                But all the same. No, gentlemen, please. I
                didn't mean it. I never said anything. Help!

He runs away from the Tsar. The Tsar pursues.

UBU   Holy shit, this dumb moron is gaining on
                me! What am I gonna do now? Oh – phew
                – there's the moat of the American camp!
                Can I make it across? He's right behind me,
                the pathetic phony! I gotta jump!

*He jumps the moat, and makes it across. The Tsar, mere feet
behind, slips.*

TSAR   *(in moat)*
               Bollocks!

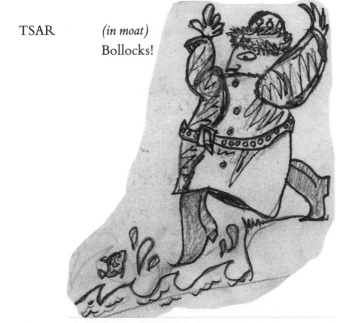

AMERICANS The Tsar is in the moat! Make
America great again!

UBU   Aha! I dared leap, and now make my
               triumphant re-entry into the American
               camp! And look who's fallen right in it!
               Pathetic! Loser! (*to soldiers*) C'mon, my
               fans, why don't you throw some stones or
               something – he's a big enough target –
               yeah, you should probably hit the gym,
               huh? My prediction was totally right. The
               golf iron was the right way forward.
               There's no doubt I would've completely
               killed him, if it weren't for that very
               inexplicable loss of courage which suddenly
               came across me – I must be ill. No,
               poisoned. In fact, it was astonishing that
               I managed to take him on at all. It was
               sadly necessary for me to run away, in order
               that I wasn't caught, which would have
               been a pathetic sign of weakness. I like
               veterans who aren't captured. Anyway, it all
               turned out marvellously. I couldn't have
               asked for more. Is anyone paying any
               attention to me?

*The Russian dragoons have charged. Some attack, while others
efficiently pull the Tsar out of the moat.*

GENERAL   This time it's a rout! Help!

UBU   (*mocking*) Ooh! A rout! You loser! (*prepares to flee*) Well, he's the expert – I'm not sticking around if he's not.

AMERICAN SOLDIERS It's every man for himself! Again.

UBU   Let's get out of here. What a failure! What failures these people are! You're in my way! Hey, you pushed me! Watch out for your King! I'm going to have you locked up! Quick, I'm going to get out of here, while the General's back is turned.

Exit Ubu. Onstage, we see the Tsar process through the battlefield, as the Russian army pursues the last few fleeing Americans.

SCENE V

A cave in Lithuania
UBU, and his Trumpeters TRITE and TRILLANY.

UBU   This weather is a disaster. I thought it was global warming we were supposed to be getting – am I right? I'm freezing to death! Something is very wrong with this country!

TRITE   Sir, haven't you gotten over losing the war, your country, your wife and all your money yet?

UBU   I'm not scared of anything! However, I
             judge it sensible never to return to America.
             Ever.

TRILLANY   *(aside)* Terrible. He's a total mess.

UBU   Hey, Mr Trillany! What are you doing over
             there, biting your nails? You scared or
             something?

TRILLANY   As well, Sir, as could be expected,
             considering that we're expecting to have an
             increasingly short future.

UBU   Well, thanks for the positivity! You always
             were a loser. Me, on the other hand, I
             displayed the greatest bravery, and without
             causing danger to myself, I made sure that
             a great many of my enemies died. And I'm
             not even counting the people I killed *before*
             I was King...

TRITE   Trillany, do you know what happened to
             Little Donald, the kid who won the race at
             the White House?

TRILLANY   He got a bullet to the head.

UBU   Ah! Just as the rose and the lily of the
             field are cut down by the vicious efforts
             of the vicious mower who mows the lawn
             viciously, so he was cut down by the

vicious Russians! Oh, Little Donald – you were strong, but the Russians were stronger.

TRITE & TRILLANY Poor Donald.

ECHO   Old...oh...oh...

TRITE   Christ! What was that?

UBU   Oh, just some more Russians, I bet! I've had enough! Something has got to change around here! Bottom line: if they piss me off any more, I'll destroy 'em.

SCENE VI
The same. Enter a bear.

TRITE   Hey, Mr King!!!

UBU   Oh! Hey, look at that little guy. What a friendly face.

TRILLANY   Oh God, watch out! What an enormous bear – my ass!!!

UBU   That's a bear! Oh my God, the nasty creature! Oh, he's gonna eat me!

Protect me! No, it's okay, it's Trite he's
gone for. Phew. I can breathe again.

*The bear has wandered over to Trite and is slowly
chewing on Trite's legs. Trillany creeps up behind it, and attacks it
with a knife. Ubu takes refuge behind a rock.*

TRILLANY   To me, Trite! To me!
            Help me, Sir!

UBU   Sad. You've got to fight
            your own battles, my
            friend! Sad.

TRILLANY   I have him!

TRITE   Hold tight, Trillany! He's beginning to
            loosen his grip.

UBU   Our Father, which art in heaven...

TRILLANY   C'mon, you filthy animal!

TRITE   Ah! He's squeezing me! Crap! Sir, help us!

UBU   ...Hallowed be thy name...

TRILLANY   I've succeeded in wounding him!

TRITE   Hurrah! He bleeds!

The Trumpeters continue to struggle, the bear howls and groans, and Ubu drones on and on in prayer.

TRILLANY   Hold him for a minute, so I can get in with my explosive left hook.

UBU   ...Give us this day our daily steak 'n chips...

TRITE   Are you ready, already?

UBU   ...And forgive us our trespasses, and make sure everyone else gets what's coming to 'em...

TRILLANY   Gotcha!

He hits the bear with his explosive left hook. Huge noise of explosion. The bear drops dead.

TRITE & TRILLANY Victory!

UBU   Thank you very, very, very much, Amen. Okay, so is he dead? Can I come down off this rock yet?

TRITE   *(disgusted)* Do as you like.

UBU   *(descending)* You know, you're still alive,
          and if you ever tread the soil of America
          again, you might reflect that it was all
          due to your King, here, who practically
          killed himself praying, fasting and freezing
          on top of a blasted rock, for your sake. I
          handled the spiritual protection with as
          much courage as this gentleman *(gestures
          to Trillany)* did with his so-called left hook.
          In fact, I pushed even further with my
          determination to protect you, because I
          wasn't afraid to climb up a high mountain
          (gestures to rock) and say my prayers from
          there, in order that my prayers had less far
          to go to reach Heaven.

TRITE   You're inconceivably revolting.

UBU   Look at this pathetic little man! Thanks
          to me, you've got something to eat! I once
          heard some crazy story about a bunch
          of Greeks who hid inside a horse's
          stomach, or something – I bet my bottom
          dollar they would've been happier to fill
          their own stomachs, like us!

TRITE   Well, I'm dying of hunger here. What is
          there to eat?

TRILLANY   The bear!

UBU   What! You're gonna eat it like that –
uncooked? You savages! We need a fire.

TRILLANY   Don't we have our rifle flints?

UBU   I hate to admit it, but you're right.
And look, over there there's a little wood
where there has to be some dry branches.
Go on then, Mr Trite. Once again, I've
saved the day!

Trite stumbles off through the snow.

TRILLANY   And now, Sir, go ahead and cut up the
bear.

UBU   I'm not touching that thing – it might
not be dead yet. You cut it – you're already
half-eaten and half-dead; you're made
for the job. Meanwhile, I'll do the
important work of lighting the fire once
that loser brings back the wood.

Trillany grudgingly begins to cut up the bear.

UBU   Oh! Be careful! It moved!

TRILLANY   Sir, it's already stiff.

UBU   Hm, well, it would be better if you could cut it up faster, then, before it gets too tough to eat. We don't want Royal Indigestion.

TRILLANY   *(aside)* The rancid, two-faced toad…
                 (to Ubu) Well, Sir if you could help me out here, I could get it done much faster.

UBU   No, I don't want to! I'm sleepy!

TRITE   *(re-entering)* That snow is incredible! It's like the North Pole out there! Night's falling fast, it'll be dark in an hour. Let's hurry while we can still see.

UBU   Yeah, hear that, Trillany? Get a move on. Both of you, get a move on! Cut the beast up and cook him! I'm starving!

TRILLANY   This is too much! I've had enough of you. You're going to help cook, or you're going to get nothing, you hear me?

UBU   Oh! Well it's all the same to me – I was happy to eat it raw, it was you two who were fussy about cooking it. Anyway, I'm too exhausted to cook it.

TRITE   Look, Trillany, what shall we do? Eat

dinner ourselves and give him nothing? Or we could give him the bones.

TRILLANY   Fine. Ah, the fire's caught.

UBU   That's all well and good. At least I'll finally be warm. Wait! Was that the Russians? I think I can see them...the Russians... Bordure... *(he falls asleep mid-sentence.)*

TRITE   *(whispering)* I want to find out if what the General said was true: that Mama Ubu has been kicked out of the White House. It's not impossible.

TRILLANY   Finish your dinner.

TRITE   No, this is more important. We need to establish the truth of these reports.

TRILLANY   The choice is this: abandon Ubu now, or stay and take care of him?

TRITE   Aw, I don't know. Let's sleep on it. *Que sera, sera.*

TRILLANY   No! We should take advantage of cover of darkness if we want to leave.

TRITE   Okay, jeez, let's go.

They creep away.

SCENE VII
The same.

UBU   *(talking in his sleep)* Ah! Well, Mr Russian Dragoon, pay attention. You're shooting into the crowd. Ah! Captain Bordure was the bear, in disguise! And Buggerlaw is coming towards me...! The bear, the bear! Aaaaah! I don't wanna. Go 'way, Buggerlaw. You think you're so funny. Now here's the General, and the Tsar...help, stop beating me! And my wife! Where have you taken all my money? You've taken my money away, you mean bitch, you've stolen it from my tomb...I've been dead a long time, and it was him, Buggerlaw, that killed me and shut me up in this asshole coffin next to fucking Wenceslas, and also in Russia next to all the Tsars, and also in that dumb cave next to the

bear, and also in the dungeon next
to Bordure. There's Bordure again.
Go 'way, you fucking bear. You look like
Bordure. D'you hear me, you lying beast
of Satan? No, he can't hear, the Trumpeters
have cut off his ears. Slaughter them
all! Cut off their ears! Take their money!
And drink yourself to death! That's the life
of my followers, and a happy life it is...

END OF
ACT IV

ACT V
SCENE I
The cave.

Night. UBU, sleeping. MAMA UBU enters without seeing him.
Utter darkness.

MAMA UBU At last, shelter! I am alone, but that's
no bad thing. But what a journey, across
Europe on foot, like a bum! Everything
bad that could have happened, happened.
As soon as that gross lemon left for
Russia, I got to the crypt to find the gold.
Then as soon as I get my hands on it,
Buggerlaw and his goons turn up and
stone me almost to death. I lost my body-
guard, Trashtag, who was so enthralled by
my beauty that he used to faint with joy
whenever he saw me – and often, he
confessed, when he didn't see me – which
is the height of love. And in the end it was
true that he had to lay down his life for me
– he was sliced in two by Buggerlaw.
Pah! What's the use of carrying on, in this
disastrous situation? And then, I took
flight, chased by the enraged mob. Had
to leave the palace without any of my
jewellery or makeup, arrived at the airport
to find they weren't letting anyone through,
had to stow away on a cruise ship and
survive by stealing from the fruit platters

they left out in the first-class lounge! I
thought I'd be caught a thousand times, I've
had nothing to eat or drink for four
days, Buggerlaw has a full international
warrant for my arrest, I didn't dare stop in
all this snow – but at last, I can rest!
Ouch, my feet! And all my nails are broken.
Well, I'd really like to know what's
happened to my esteemed spouse. After all,
did I steal his money? Did I take one cent?
Did I get one lousy bean for myself out of
this? I'm like his horse, that died of
hunger. Huh! It's a story of true devotion.
And I lost my treasure. Well, at least nobody knows where it is. It's safe in the
Royal crypt, stashed inside the tomb
of Laidislaw the Great.

UBU   *(beginning to wake up)* ...and capture that
             bitch of a wife of mine, cut off her toenails!

MAMA UBU Oh my Lord! Where have I landed up? I
             heard my husband's voice! I must be losing
             my mind!
             I heard a bump,
             And saw a fat lump,
             Monsieur Ubu – *thump*!
             Let's be nice. Here goes. Sir, did you sleep
             well?

UBU   Fuck off, Trillany! That bear gave me
               indigestion! I guess our fight was a battle of
               tooth and claw, in which the tooth won.
               Or rather, the stomach. Ha, ha! The
               stomach! I am pretty funny, aren't I. What
               do you think of that, Trumpeters? A battle
               of stomach and claw?

MAMA UBU What's he gibbering on about? He's even
               more irritating than I remember. Who's he
               talking to?

UBU   Trite, Trillany, answer me, you sacks of
               shit! Where are you? Oh! I'm scared! What
               was that? Did someone say something?
               Well, at least it's not the bear, I guess. Shit!
               Where are my glasses? Oh yeah, I lost them
               in the battle.

MAMA UBU *(aside)* I'm gonna make the best of
               this darkness. I'll pretend to be a ghost, and
               scare him into promising me a portion of
               his wealth.

UBU   Someone definitely said something over
               there. Oh, I'm going to die, all alone!

MAMA UBU *(in a deep voice)* Yes, Ubu, it was I that
               spoke, and the Last Trump that will awake
               the dead on the Day of Judgement is no

more mighty a voice! Listen well to my words, for they are those of the Archangel Gabriel, and they are wisdom indeed.

UBU   Shit! No fear!

MAMA UBU   Don't interrupt me when I'm talking! Or I'll shut you up by removing your vocal chords.

UBU   Not my vocal chords! I won't say another word. Go on!

MAMA UBU   We know, Ubu, that you are a fat bastard.

UBU   Very fat, that's right, sir, I'm a hideous bastard.

MAMA UBU   Shut up, for Chrissake!

UBU   Oh, I didn't know angels took the Lord's name in vain!

MAMA UBU   *(aside)* Jesus! *(to Ubu)* Are you married, Ubu?

UBU   Absolutely, to Frankenstein's monster.

MAMA UBU   It was only a little rhinoplasty! You mean, to a beautiful and charming woman.

UBU   No, she's a bitch. She's always hormonal,
and she isn't even that hot any more.
I dunno what to do with her.

MAMA UBU   What you'll do with her, you fat ass, is
treat her with some respect! And if you
did, she might be a little less grumpy.

UBU   Who's getting some rumpy-pumpy?

MAMA UBU   You aren't listening, Ubu, concentrate a
little. *(Aside)* I must hurry, the sun is
rising! Ubu, your wife is adorable,
delicious, a Venus, and she doesn't have a
single flaw.

UBU   That's a lie. There isn't a single flaw she
doesn't have.

MAMA UBU   Silence! Your wife is entirely loyal and
has never been unfaithful to you!

UBU   I'd like to know who'd be willing to fuck
her with a face like that!

MAMA UBU   She never drinks!

UBU   Yeah, since I changed the locks on the
cellars. Before that, she stank of eau-de-vie
at seven in the morning, and couldn't walk

in a straight line till midday sherry. Now she reeks of Chanel No. 5, which isn't much better. But at least I'm the only one who can get to my wine!

MAMA UBU   You bastard – ! Your wife has never taken any money from you.

UBU   No. Ha, ha, ha!

MAMA UBU   She's not taken a cent!

UBU   Yeah – she's like my old horse, that wasn't fed for three months, dragged me all the way to Russia, and dropped dead! Ha, ha, ha! Poor beast.

MAMA UBU   Everything bad said about her is a
                       lie, false news and unprofessional reporting.
                       Your wife is an angel, and you are a
                       monster!

UBU   Yeah, I can't deny it. My wife's pretty
                       dumb. Why do you care?

MAMA UBU   Take care, Ubu.

UBU   Oh yeah, sorry, I forgot who I was
                       speaking to. I didn't say anything! It was a
                       lie!

MAMA UBU   You killed Wenceslas.

UBU   It wasn't my fault. That's a disgraceful lie.
                       Very unprofessional. Sad.

MAMA UBU   You killed Boleslaw and Laidislaw.

UBU   Too bad! They should have been tougher.

MAMA UBU   You broke your promises to Bordure,
                       and later you killed him.

UBU   I preferred that it was me who had control
                       of California – what's so bad about that?
                       Anyway, that's a lie too.

MAMA UBU   There's only one way all your evildoings
           can be pardoned.

UBU   How? I am a good person. I'm very keen
           to be a saint, one day. I'd like to see my
           name on the calendar.

MAMA UBU   You have to forgive Mama Ubu for
           taking some of America's money.

UBU   Huh! Sure, I'll forgive her when she's given
           it all back and more, and I've thrashed her
           within an inch of her life, and she's brought
           my horse back to life.

MAMA UBU   He's obsessed with that horse. And I've
           failed! The sun is rising.

UBU   Well, I'm glad you let me know my wife
           has been fleecing me. I needed to know
           from someone honourable. God knows,
           God knows it all, eh? You don't look very
           cheery, Miss Ghostly Lady, c'mon, give us
           a smile? How about a cuddle? Look, the
           sun is rising! Ah, God, it's my wife!

MAMA UBU   *(terrified)* No it's not! And now you're
           going to hell!

UBU   Ah! You bitch!

MAMA UBU Swearing at an archangel? How dare you!

UBU I can see your own horse-face, you stupid cow! Why the hell are you here?

MAMA UBU Trashtag was killed and the Americans chased me out.

UBU Well, I got chased by the biggest army in the world – the Russian. We have so much in common!

MAMA UBU Apart from the fact that I'm beautiful and you're a pig.

UBU You're asking for a bearhug, ma'am! *(he heaves the remains of the bear up and throws them at her.)*

MAMA UBU *(falling over from the bear's weight)* My God! He's killed me! I'm choking! Fuck! It's suffocating me!

UBU Ew, gross. Is she dead yet? Perhaps not. Better pray. Our Father…*(as he clambers back on the rock.)*

MAMA UBU *(pulling herself out from under the bearhide)* Sheesh! Where is he?

UBU   Oh my God, still here? You crooked bitch, there's no way to destroy you. Is the bear definitely dead?

MAMA UBU   Of course, you ginger moron, it's only a skin. How did it get here?

UBU   *(confused)* I'm not sure...Ah, I remember! It wanted to eat Trite and Trillany, so I killed it by praying.

MAMA UBU   Trite, Trillany, praying? What is all this? He's delusional.

UBU   It's true. It is so true. And you, you are a lying, crooked, lying bitch, I swear.

MAMA UBU   Tell me about how your European deals went, Ubu.

UBU   Oh, hell, that's a long story. All I know is, it was rigged. Those losers had it in for me.

MAMA UBU   What, even the American people?

UBU   They were yelling: 'Go Wenceslas and Buggerlaw! We want change!' You know, I think they really wanted to destroy me, those radical wackos! Sad! And they even got Little Donald!

MAMA UBU   Who cares about your little Ub-a-thon media mascot? You hear they got Trashtag?

UBU   Who cares about him? And then they killed the poor, little General! I loved that guy.

MAMA UBU   Who cares!

UBU   Honey, how about you get on your knees to your betters and say that to my face instead of hiding behind some rocks, huh? You should get on your knees. *(He hesitates, then rushes over to her, and forces her to kneel.)* Heel! I'm in full support of reinstating the death penalty in our great country.

MAMA UBU   Ha ha, I don't care, I hate you, you fool!

UBU   Oho! You finished yet? Okay, so let me begin: twisting your nose off, pulling out your armpit hair one hair at a time, extracting your brain through your nostrils with a hook, whipping your ass, chemical injections to the spine, if that'll make you any less spiky, not forgetting the operation to remove your bladder, splinters under

your fingernails (as usual), and, finally,
decapitation à la Saint John the Baptist, the
whole set-up taken straight outta the
Old Testament, and the New, very patriotic
and holy, ordered by me, corrected by me,
perfected by me, the richest and cleverest
man in the world! How's that for you,
honey?

With that, he leaps upon her, magnificently.

MAMA UBU Mercy, Ubu!

Suddenly, a loud noise at the entrance to the cave…

SCENE II

*UBU, MAMA UBU, Then, BUGGERLAW, running into the
cave accompanied by soldiers.*

BUGGERLAW Forward, friends! For America!

UBU   Oh crap! Wait a second, Mr American, sir.
            Wait till I've finished with my other half
            here!

BUGGERLAW *(slapping him)* Get down, you balding,
            beggardly, bullying bitch!

UBU   *(indignant)* Hey! Bully yourself!

MAMA UBU *(marching over to Ubu and also giving him a slap)* You fake-tanned, fake-news, fake-businessman, pig!

The soldiers rush at the Ubs, who defend themselves as best they can.

UBU   Sheesh! What a kicking!

MAMA UBU These Americans sure have feet!

UBU   I swear, by the hair on my head, this has got to stop. Hey! I said stop it!

BUGGERLAW Hit 'em, hit 'em!

VOICE FROM OFFSTAGE Long live Ubu! Make America great again!

UBU   Thank God, reinforcements! Hurrah! Here come the Trumpeters! Gentlemen, hurry, we're in tremendous trouble!

Enter the Trumpeters and several soldiers, who hurl themselves into the fray.

TRILLANY   Get out, all you who call yourselves American!

TRITE   Hey, Mr King, we meet again...now push at the door, as hard as you can, so we trap 'em inside the cave! Once they're inside, all we have to do is run away.

UBU   Oh. I'm an expert at that. Ow, they really gave me a kicking.

BUGGERLAW *(in the cave):* God! I'm bleeding!

ADVISOR I   It's only a scratch, sir.

BUGGERLAW Yeah, it gave me a shock, that's all.

ADVISOR II Push forward, forward! They're gaining, those assholes are gaining!

TRILLANY   We're almost there – follow me, everyone! I see the light!

TRITE   Courage, Mr King!

UBU   I'm shitting in my pants! Run faster, why
                don't you! Kill 'em, slay 'em, destroy 'em,
                assert yourselves! Hey, they're backing off!

TRILLANY   There's only two guarding the doors!

UBU   (picking up the bear carcass and, swinging it
                around, stunning the guards with it) And a one!
                And a two! Oof! We've got out, and saved
                ourselves, and live!

                          SCENE III
                Lithuanian scene, in the snow.
        THE UBS, Trumpeters and Followers in flight.

UBU   I think they've given up chasing us.
                Pathetic! Weak!

MAMA UBU   Yeah, because Buggerlaw's gone to be
                inaugurated as King.

UBU   And, you know, I don't envy him the
                responsibility.

MAMA UBU   Well, you're right, for once.

They plod off into the landscape.

SCENE IV

*The deck of a ship, moving fast over the Baltic sea. On the
bridge, UBU, MAMA UBU, SHIP'S CAPTAIN and
the merry band of Trumpeters.*

SOLDIER   Ah! The feeling of the breeze ruffling
             my hair!

UBU   It's a fact that we're making tremendous
             progress. This speed has never been seen
             before! We've got to be making a million
             knots an hour. It's true – even the wind
             supports Ubu.

TRITE   What a sad imbecile he is.

*Suddenly, the wind rises. The ship pitches to one side, tossing in
white-capped waves.*

UBU   Oh, crap! We're capsized! Your crappy boat
             is going to take us all down with it!

SHIP'S CAPTAIN Everyone get downwind. Raise
             the mainsail!

UBU   Hell, no! We're not all on the same side,
             here! That's stupid. Suppose the wind
             changes? Everyone'll tip the boat and we'll
             be fast food for the fishes.

SHIP'S CAPTAIN That's not going to happen, I can
            assure you.

UBU   Yeah! Yeah! Come on. I'm under pressure,
            here – just listen to me. This fuck-up we're
            in is all your fault, Captain, and it's your
            fault if we don't get home safe. This boat
            needs strong leadership. Why aren't you
            turning? Why isn't anyone lowering that
            thing? Helm up, hoist the sails, you know!
            Yeah, that's very good, see, now we're
            cooking with gas.

*The boat lurches and everyone roars with fear. The wind becomes a
fully-flown gale.*

SHIP'S CAPTAIN Haul the jib! Take a reef into the
            topsail!

UBU   Yeah, haul, take in! Not bad, not bad.
            Listen, guys, haul on your cocks and take
            in your titties.

His followers collapse with laughter. A wave washes onboard.

UBU   Oh, what a downpour! It's all because of
            my sins!

MAMA UBU (*to TRITE*): Doesn't that look great:
            being the person in charge of where we're
            going?

Second wave washes on deck.

TRITE   Satan, I defy thee!

UBU   Can we take a break already? My legs are
killing me…

All gather around, and sit down.

MAMA UBU Ah! Isn't it nice to think that we'll shortly
be in France, enjoying a glass or two of
wine?

UBU   We'll get there soon enough! And we'll go
straight to that Buckingham place when
we land.

TRILLANY I feel rejuvenated just by the thought of
seeing dear old Spain again.

TRITE   Oh, and telling all our foreign friends all
about our adventures!

UBU   Yeah, yeah – and when I'm named Grand
European Financial Emperor in Notre-
Dame, in Paris!

MAMA UBU There's France! Oof, what a jolt!

TRITE   It's nothing. There's a light!

TRILLANY   And now, our noble vessel speeds
             at top speed across the white-crested
             wavelets of the North European sea...

UBU   Asshole sea, more like. I never wanted to
             visit Germany in the first place. I heard it's
             called that because our Germanic cousins
             live there.

MAMA UBU   That's what I call erudite. Wow, now
             isn't that beach beautiful?

UBU   Now, gentlemen, isn't that a sight to see –
             the EU! – better than any in the USA? If we
             don't have America, at least they don't have us!

THE END.

ALFRED JARRY (1873-1907)

was a playwright and one of the most significant French Symbolists. His best-known play, *Ubu Roi*, heralded the arrival of Surrealism and the Theatre of the Absurd when it appeared in 1888, later inspiring Picasso, Burroughs, Beckett and an American encyclopaedia of the avant-garde, ubuweb.com, among others. It formed an introduction to the Surrealist and Dadaist movements which were to influence the shape of twentieth-century art to come.

ROSANNA HILDYARD

is an editor and writer. Her fiction and non-fiction has been published in *The Isis Magazine*, *The Evening Press*, *The Northern Echo*, and anthologies of political writing including Oxford University's *Adrift* and *Outside Of Me* and Eyewear's *Tactical Reading: A Snappy Guide to the Snap General Election 2017*. She was winner of The Isis 500 Words competition, and writes as part of several collectives.